4 You! Mag[azine]

by Jillian Po[well]

Contents

Section 1

Who Says the Camera Never Lies?	2
Astrology on the Net	6

Section 2

Your Letters	8
So You Want to Be a Driver!	11
Give Your Bedroom a Feng-shui Makeover	17

Section 3

The Great Escape: Holidays Without the Grown-ups	22
Adopt a Tiger!	28

Edinburgh Gate
Harlow, Essex

Who Says the Camera Never Lies?

Clever Camera Tricks

So you've got your new camera. You've taken some photos of your family and friends, and one of your pet pooch too.

Now it's **really time** to have some fun!

Circus Acts

Try taking a picture of a friend so it looks as if a tree is growing out of his head! Your friend must stand in front of you with the tree behind him. Look through your camera and make sure you can see the tree straight above your friend's head. You may need to move, or ask your friend to move around to get the best shot. You can use tall buildings or chimneys instead of trees.

Ask a friend to stand in front of a wall or a gatepost. It needs to be about the same height that your friend is. Find an object like a beach ball or a tall vase and place it on the wall just above her head. Now stand back and shoot your picture.

Get one friend to stand on a stool and hold his arms out as if he is on a tightrope. Ask another friend to crouch down in front of the stool. Ask her to put her hands by her shoulders with the palms facing upwards. She must look as if she is carrying something really heavy. Stand back so you can't see the stool and shoot!

Monsters and Ghosts

Get two friends to dress up in white clothes and put talcum powder or a white face mask on their faces. Ask one to hide behind the other and put her arms around the friend in front's waist. Have the four arms doing different things like reading or playing a musical instrument.

Ask your friend to dress up in a white sheet. Now try scrunching up some cling film and put it carefully over the lens of your camera. Shoot the picture through the cling film.

Ask a friend to stand outside a window and press his face against the glass. Shoot the picture through the window.

Take a picture indoors after dark. If your camera has auto-flash, take out the battery. Help your friend put on a green face mask. Then shine a torch underneath her face. Ask her to pull a monster face. Scary!

UFOs

Find some plastic picnic saucers. Choose a window which has a view of a garden and some sky. Stick the saucers to the window using blobs of Blu-tack so that the saucers look as if they are flying through the sky.

Reflections and Shadows

Try taking pictures of people or buildings reflected in water, mirrors or other shiny surfaces. This can make them look strange or mysterious. There is usually one best angle, so check it out before you shoot.

> **Try:**
> 📷 buildings or trees reflected in water
> 📷 a friend reflected in a car's hubcap
> 📷 fairground mirrors for weird reflections.

On a sunny day, try shooting pictures of shadows of people, buildings or objects. The early morning or late afternoon sun gives the best shadows.

Crazy Collage

You can make a collage of cut-outs from your own photos or pictures cut out of newspapers and magazines. Cut out pictures of people and objects. Try to choose them so they are lots of different sizes. Now have fun arranging them on a large piece of card or thick paper. You could have someone sitting in an egg cup or a huge dog taking a small person for a walk!

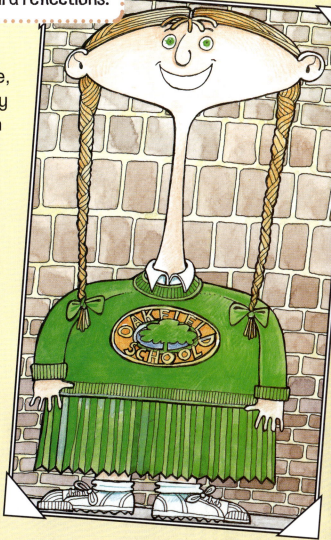

Astrology on the Net

Do you want to check your daily or monthly horoscope? Or find out which star sign your favourite footballer or popstar is? Well, the Internet has all the answers! Check out these web sites to find out everything from your Chinese birth sign to David Beckham's astrological chart.

The Club at **www.ncbuy.com/entertainment/astrology/**

Here you can check on your daily or monthly horoscope, or check out a friend's horoscope, then e-mail it to him or her.

Astrology for the Real World at **www.claruss.demon.co.uk** gives charts for celebrities including footballers Michael Owen and David Beckham.

Russell Grant at **www.russellgrant.com** is packed with stars and features by the popular astrologer.

Astrobytes at **www.astronet.com**
Look up your horoscope and find out which star signs make the best friends and partners for you.

www.planet.eon.net/~tgradi/astroweb.html
The site to give you an introduction to Chinese astrology. Chinese astrologers believe that the year of your birth decides your future. There are 12 birth signs including the Year of the Cat, the Dog, the Monkey and the Tiger. Find out what your birth sign is and look up some celebrity horoscopes.

Mood Gel
The hair gel that changes colour with your mood

Mood Gel is a new kind of hair gel. It reacts with your body chemistry to change colour.
So if you're feeling wild, your hair can look that way too ... make your hair as unpredictable as you are. Try **Mood Gel**.

Your Letters

Professor Brayne Box answers your letters.

Dear Professor B. Box

Which is the biggest selling games console – Sega Mega Drive, or Nintendo Game Boy?

Answer:

Nintendo Game Boy has sold more than any other console, but watch out for Sega's Dreamcast.

Dear Professor B. Box

Who owns the Internet and who invented it?

Answer:

No one owns the Net. People and organisations who use the Internet own their computers and cables and together they make up the Net. The US Defense Department developed the Net in the late 1960s. It wanted to make sure that if part of the US computer network was destroyed by bombs in a nuclear attack, information could still be sent around the country. If they could not send information direct from A to B, they could still send it from A to C, then from C to B.

Dear Professor B. Box
Which dinosaurs could run the fastest?

Answer:

The fastest dinosaurs were the ornithomimids. They were egg-eating dinosaurs that raided the nests of other dinosaurs. They had very long back legs and may have run as fast as 80 kilometres per hour.

Dear Professor B. Box
What was the first ever science-fiction film?

Answer:

The earliest science-fiction movie was made in 1903. It was based on a novel by Jules Verne. It was called *A Trip to the Moon*, and the director was George Melies.

Dear Professor B. Box
When did martial arts first become a sport?

Answer:

Martial arts are based on methods of combat and self defence used by Japanese warriors called Samurai from the 1600s onwards. They include judo, karate, aikido and sumo. They developed into sports in Japan about 100 years ago.

Dear Professor B. Box
How old is the Space Shuttle?
Answer:
The first Space Shuttle was launched in 1981 using the vehicle *Columbia*.

Dear Professor B. Box
How can bats fly if they are blind?
Answer:
Bats have very poor eyesight but they use sound waves to 'see'. They make high squeaking noises from their mouths or noses that humans can't hear. These sounds bounce off objects and send back echoes that the bat can hear. Bats can use the echoes to find flying insects to eat.

Dear Professor B. Box
Which is the biggest selling pop group in history?
Answer:
The 1960s' 'Fab Four' — the Beatles are the only group to have sold more than a billion recordings!

So You Want to Be a Driver!

You don't have to be 17 before you can start practising your driving skills. Take a look at some ways to get behind the wheel before you get your L Plates!

Karting Karting Karting Karting

You can try your hand at driving by Pro-karting at an indoor or outdoor circuit. The circuit hires out karts and all the safety equipment you need. Pro-karting will give you a head start for outdoor circuit racing.

You can get started by sending for a Start Karting Pack from the Motorsports Association (MSA). This includes information on rules and regulations and a video about the sport. You then need to find your nearest Racing Kart School by contacting the Association of Racing Kart Schools (ArkS). You will need some lessons to prepare you for the ArkS driving test. Once you have passed your test, you can send for your Karting licence. Then you just need to join a Karting club to start racing!

Boys and girls can start karting from the age of 8 upwards – 8–12-year-olds race in the Formula Cadet Class. You race specially built karts with 2 stroke, 60 cc Comer engines. The Association of British Race Kart Clubs (AbkC) run kart clubs all over the country. By joining an AbkC club, you can race at any of the Association's circuits, and take part in the AbkC Championships. The MSA runs a Cadet British Championship as part of its Champions of the Future Series.

Karts can be hired but you will need safety clothing before you can race. Look in karting magazines and small ads in newspapers to find used equipment. You will need a crash helmet approved for racing, a racing suit, gloves and boots that protect your ankles. Some clubs have equipment for hire.

Karting Facts

- Many famous racing drivers, including Ayrton Senna, started their careers by karting.
- The kart was invented in California in 1956 by Art Ingels, a racing car mechanic, and his friend Lou Borelli. They found some spare 100 cc lawnmower engines and made a simple frame using steel tubes and four wheels.
- The first kart racing track was built at Azusa in California.

Further Information

The Association of British Kart Clubs (ABkC) at
http://www.karting.co.uk/ABkC
Or contact the Secretary, Graham Smith, tel. 01926 812177, e-mail address **graham.smith@mcmail.com**

The Association of Racing Kart Schools at
http://www.ARKS.co.uk

Start Karting Pack, available from Motorsports Association, Motorsports House, Riverside Park, Colnbrook, Slough SL3 0HG, tel. 01753 681736

Karting Magazine, and further karting information, including the book Cadet Kart Racing, available from Lodgemark Press, Bark House, Summerhill, Chislehurst, Kent BR7 5RD

Racing games games games games

Video and computer games let you practise your driving skills at home. Steering wheels come with gas and brake pedals and have gear sticks or shift paddles to change gears. Some have 'Rumble Paks' which shake in your hands as you take sharp corners! Most computer games are races, like Gran Turismo or Driver.
You can watch replays after each race to try to improve your driving skills.

Some to try:
- Top Gear Rally
- Metropolis Street Racer
- Colin McRae Rally
- Formula 1 Racing
- Toca 2 Touring Cars
- Sega Rally 2

You can even practise taking your driving test using computer software. 'Driving and Theory Tests' tests you in real-life driving situations such as motorways and emergencies, and checks out your knowledge of the Highway Code. You can also practise taking your theory test and get feedback on your answers.

Zip...
the trainers with *attitude*

Zip is the new word in trainers. Zip use online technology to customise your trainers. You choose the style. You choose the colour. You choose the logo. You design your trainers. We make them. You wear them!

Zip trainers online @ **www.zip.onlinetrainers.com**

Give Your Bedroom a Feng-shui Makeover

What is Feng-shui?

Feng-shui is about 4000 years old. It began in Ancient China but is now practised all over the world. Feng-shui means 'wind and water'. It's pronounced 'fong shway'.

Feng-shui is a cross between an art and a science. Its goal is to arrange buildings, rooms and furniture in the best way to create harmony with nature. Feng-shui experts believe that the way we arrange our surroundings can bring us happiness, health and good luck. They believe we can improve the flow of chi, which is the energy found in people, the Earth and the Universe.

Improve Your Own Chi

You can improve your own chi by practising some feng-shui rules in your bedroom. Feng-shui experts believe the bedroom is an important room because we spend about a third of our lives in bed! It can also be the place where you work, play and entertain your friends.

Start by clearing away any clutter. An untidy room is bad feng-shui and clutter can block the flow of good chi. For a good night's sleep, it is better to place your bed away from doors and windows. If you can, move your bed to the opposite corner from your bedroom door. This will give you the best view of your room and let you see anyone who comes in. If you can't move the bed, hang a mirror so you can see your bedroom door when you are in bed.

Desks should also be facing the door. If you put your desk in the north-east corner of your room, it can help your studies! Computers are good and bring energy to your room but set them up so you can see the bedroom door when you are working on them.

Posters of your favourite people or places can inspire you. Put a poster of your favourite rock or movie star on a north wall if you want a career in films or music. Choose the south wall if you want fame, or the south-east wall if you want wealth! (Use a compass to find out which is north, south, east and west in your room.)

Lights and lamps represent the Sun. We need bright light to help chi flow.

An atlas globe represents the Earth. Spin it daily to stir up lucky chi. Other spinning objects like clock hands and CD players can also help stir up good chi.

Hang crystals from your window or door. They can help chi and family harmony.

The Chinese string old coins from red ribbon and hang them by a window or a wall to bring wealth. You can try stringing shiny bottle tops from red ribbon instead.

Objects that Improve Chi

- mirrors, lights, crystals
- fish, plants, flowers (but make sure you keep them alive and healthy!)
- windchimes and bells
- hanging mobiles and windmills
- computers

The Chinese believe that some colours are luckier than others. White is good for a young person's room and red is a lucky colour.

Feng-shui Animals

Many Chinese people keep fish because they are believed to bring good luck. You can keep ornaments or pictures of fish if you can't have the real thing.

If you want fame, put pictures or figures of horses in the south corner of your room. Elephants are good too, as they represent wisdom.

Feng-shui Fact

In China, many people go to a Feng-shui expert before they buy a new home.

Smelly Paints

Hate the smell of fresh paint? How about the smell of chocolate, fresh coffee or doughnuts?

Paint your room not just the colour you like but the smell you like. Choose from ten super smells and feast your senses …

The Great Escape: Holidays Without the Grown-ups

Family holidays are great, but sometimes it's good to do your own thing. Kids Camps first became popular in the USA, but now there are holidays to suit every interest and activity. Try these for size! Most can collect you from pick-up points if you are travelling on your own. They provide dormitory-style accommodation or twin or single rooms. Some can offer vegetarian and special diets.

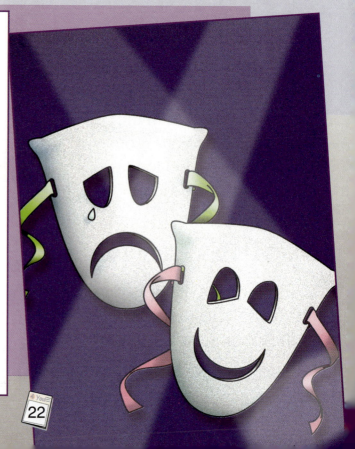

If it's bright lights and fame you seek, head for a summer drama holiday at **Centre Stage**. Based at a beautiful house in a forest park in Dungannon, 40 minutes from Belfast, the school offers courses in dance, drama, mime and make-up. All the courses are taught by professional actors. At the end of the holiday, students put on a show and hold their own Oscar ceremony!

For 8–18 years.
Tel. 01232 249119.

The junior membership of the Royal Society for the Protection of Birds (RSPB) run wildlife holidays for members and their friends throughout the year at field centres, youth hostels and private hostels. On its Island Adventure holidays, you stay at pine log-cabins on an uninhabited Scottish island. You can go seal and deer watching, as well as enjoying mud wallowing and a Robinson Crusoe survival night! There are a range of RSPB holidays for young people and their families at centres around the UK.

For young people up to 18 years old.
Tel. the RSPB on 01767 680551.

Exsportise is the brainchild of Olympic gold medallist Steve Batchelor. It runs residential sports holidays in the summer, based at a school in Surrey with hundreds of acres of sports grounds. The sports on offer include tennis, hockey, golf, swimming and cricket. Instructors are experts in their fields, including Olympic champions!

For 8–18-year-olds. Tel. 01293 862849.

For outdoor activities, the **YMCA** runs adventure holidays at centres all over the country. Activities include abseiling and rock climbing.

Contact your local **YMCA** or telephone the National Council on 020 8520 5599.

If you prefer watersports, **Calshot Activities Centre**, based on the Solent, offers multi-activity holidays in the summer, including dinghy sailing and canoeing. You must be able to swim at least 50 metres.

For 8 to 16-year-olds. Tel. 01703 8920777.

Heart of Wales Riding Holidays offers riding in the Welsh Mountains.

For 8–16-year-olds. Tel. 01597 851884.

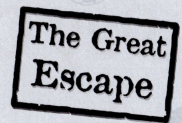

The Great Escape

PGL Adventure Holidays offers multi-activity holidays in the UK and France, with themes including Indiana Jones Adventure, motorsports, and riding and trekking.

Tel. 01989 768768.

Day Camps

If you want to try out some holiday activities, but aren't sure about staying away from home, some centres offer day camps where you can attend on a daily or weekly basis. Most arrange regular pick-ups for children travelling alone.

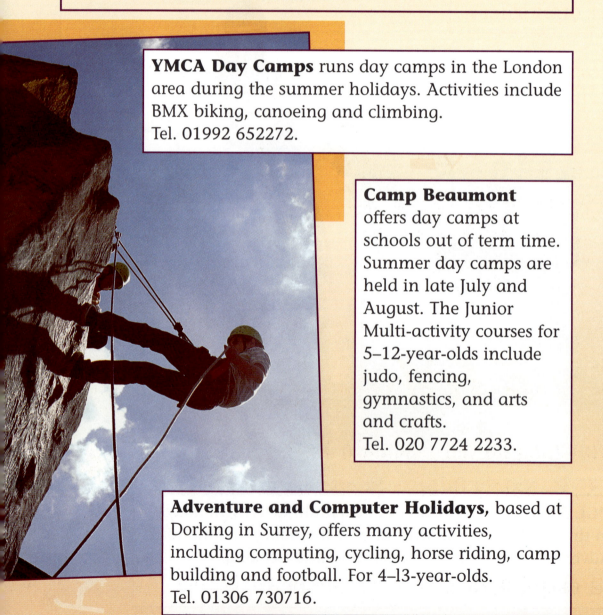

YMCA Day Camps runs day camps in the London area during the summer holidays. Activities include BMX biking, canoeing and climbing.
Tel. 01992 652272.

Camp Beaumont offers day camps at schools out of term time. Summer day camps are held in late July and August. The Junior Multi-activity courses for 5–12-year-olds include judo, fencing, gymnastics, and arts and crafts.
Tel. 020 7724 2233.

Adventure and Computer Holidays, based at Dorking in Surrey, offers many activities, including computing, cycling, horse riding, camp building and football. For 4–13-year-olds.
Tel. 01306 730716.

Action Holidays has centres around the country and offers a range of activities, including orienteering, circus skills, scavenger hunts and video film-making. For 8–11-year-olds. Tel. 01706 814554.

If you want to be the next Junior Masterchef, you could try a course at **Aspic**, a cookery school in Cambridge run by professional cook Alice Percival. Courses are held in August and October and you can take home everything you have prepared! For 9–15-year-olds. Tel. 01223 568303.

The following also offer non-residential day camps:
- Calshot Activities Centre, tel. 01703 892077
- Escapade Activity Holidays, tel. 020 8446 8837
- Exsportise, tel. 01293 862849.

Free Wheeler

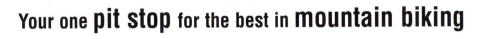

Everything for the mountain biker:
- **Kit** • **Safety Gear** • **Spare Parts** •

Your one **pit stop** for the best in **mountain biking**

Adopt a Tiger!

Sarah Leggett runs the Animals Adoption Scheme at London Zoo. JP asks her how you can become part of the scheme.

Q: What sort of people adopt an animal at the Zoo?

Sarah: *All sorts of people! Our youngest adoptive parent has only just been born, and our oldest adopter is 92. Anyone who takes an interest in animals and their welfare can become an animal adopter at London Zoo. Lots of people give adoptions as presents for birthdays or other special occasions, or simply adopt an animal for themselves. We also have lots of schools and scout and guide troops taking part in the scheme, for example, and we even have lots of celebrity adopters!*

Q: How much does it cost to adopt an animal?

Sarah: *Adoptions last for a year. It costs anything from £25 to adopt an ant up to £6000 to adopt a whole Asian elephant! But if you'd rather not adopt a whole animal, you can adopt a share in one of our larger animals for £35 — we don't specify which bit is yours!*

Q: What happens when you adopt an animal? Do you get to take it home?

Sarah: You can't take it home, but we give you a free ticket to the Zoo so that you can come and visit your adopted species! You will also receive a certificate of adoption and a photo of your adopted species. We send you Lifewatch magazine for a year and your name will be listed on our special thank-you board for a year.

Q: What sort of animals do people adopt?

Sarah: You can adopt any species that we have at London Zoo, which means there are over 600 to choose from! Our information leaflet lists some of the more popular animals for adoption, but if you would like to adopt an animal that isn't on the list, you can call to check if we have any at the Zoo.

Q: What are the most popular animals for adoption?

Sarah: Our Sumatran tiger and the black-footed penguins are always the most adopted animals, and the gorillas, Asian elephants and giraffes are very popular as well.

Q: Which are the most unusual animals that people adopt?

Sarah: One of the most unusual, yet most popular, animals is the dung beetle, which lives in and feeds on elephant dung! There are many other weird and wonderful creatures at the Zoo, and you can adopt any of them.

Q: How does the Animal Adoption Scheme help the Zoo?

Sarah: Every adoption helps pay for an animal's food, veterinary care and the upkeep of Zoo habitats. By adopting an animal, you are playing your part in animal conservation. The Zoo takes part in conservation programmes throughout the world. If you adopt a seahorse, for example, your money will go to Project Seahorse, a conservation programme which is working to save seahorses in Vietnam and the Philippines.

Q: How do people find out more about adopting an animal?

Sarah: They can write to us at London Zoo or call us on 020 7449 6262. You can also find out more information on the scheme on either of our web sites at **www.zsl.org** or **www.weboflife.co.uk**.

Q: Finally, Sarah, if you could adopt any animal, what would that be and why?

Sarah: Well, I've adopted lots of animals for friends and family, but I think it would be hard for me to choose a favourite at the Zoo! I would probably adopt something very endangered that needs lots of adopters, such as the partula snail, which is almost extinct in the wild.

Animal Adopters

The pupils at Sydenham High School in south-east London raised £500 to adopt animals at London Zoo. They held cake sales, non-uniform days and even organised a 'National Bunches' day when everyone in school paid 50 pence to wear bunches for the day. The school then held a big assembly, and each class talked about their favourite animal. The girls put all the choices into a hat to decide the winners. They decided to adopt a black-tipped reef shark, a leopard ground gecko, a Senegal bushbaby and a black-footed penguin, so they have a fish, a reptile, a mammal and a bird! The girls are now looking forward to visiting their adopted animals at the Zoo.

Some of the Animals You Can Adopt at London Zoo:

Asian elephant	Leopard	Red panda
Black rhinoceros	Sumatran tiger	Gorilla
Bushbaby	Camel	Reindeer
Two toed sloth	Shark	Chimpanzee
Chinese alligator	Giraffe	Tarantula spider
Red-faced spider monkey		Piranha fish